Citroën 2cv

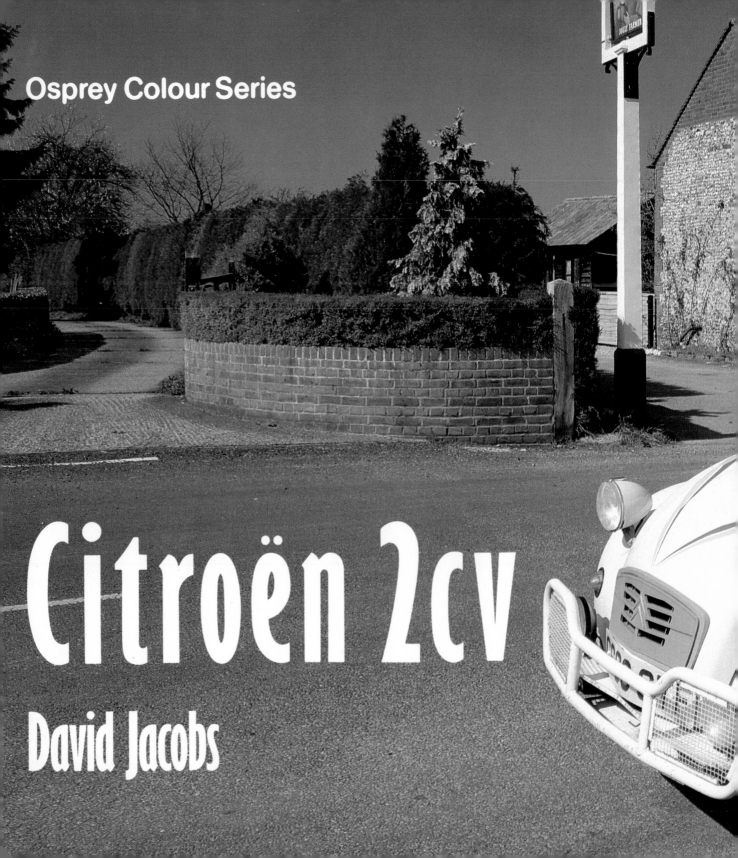

Osprey Colour Series

Citroën 2cv

David Jacobs

Contents

First published in 1989 by Osprey Publishing
59 Grosvenor Street, London W1X 9DA

© David Jacobs 1989

Editor Nicholas Collins
Designer Simon Bell
Printed in Hong Kong

British Library Cataloguing-in-Publication Data

Jacobs, David
  Citroen 2CV
  1. Citroen 2CV cars to 1980
  I. Title
  629.2'222
  ISBN 0-850-45873-0

Introduction

About the author
David Jacobs is an outstanding photographer. He has an unfailing eye for the exceptional in terms of composition and colour.

He is also a tremendous enthusiast for the automotive world. His earlier books *American Buses* and *American Trucks* (both Osprey) revealed that he is prepared to go to unusual lengths to capture the rare, the exciting and even the bizarre in roadgoing images. To consistently deliver memorable and even classic photographs reveals David's profound knowledge and love of his chosen sphere.

In this latest book, David has distilled the essence of the 2CV. David lives in Hampstead where he is known as a leading creative photographer and chronicler of the lives of the area's many characters.

Modern-day motoring is rarely a leisurely experience. Today's overcrowded roads are a nightmare: we all know the frustration of endless traffic jams, spaghetti junctions, stop signs and hazards of every description.

Yet in these difficult conditions there exists a strong non-conformist movement. The twentieth century motorist need not follow current trends: the latest show-room model, with turbocharging, power-assisted steering and the acceleration of a rocket is fine, but is its driver any better off when confronted with the inevitability of the morning rush, or crowded holiday escape routes?

A car that is both cherished by its enthusiastic owners and ridiculed by its antagonists as a 'snail on four wheels' does not go unnoticed, wherever its owner takes it, which is often along scenic B roads rather than on aggressive motorways. Now more than forty years old, this famous French road runner lives on, to the delight of its fans the world over.

A vehicle of French origin which is sadly no longer manufactured at its famous though unaccessible factory at Levallois, to the north-west of Paris, the 2CV is now produced in Portugal: its design, which has evolved at such a slow rate, ensures that it has never lost its appeal to young and old alike.

However, the two horse-powered oddity has never been

able to escape from criticism. Why the ridicule? Admittedly it has a small air-cooled engine, tortoise-paced transmission, frugal instrumentation, minimal 'refinements', even to the non-existent wind-down windows! Surely, though, the car scores points for its lack of complexity and for not being built and run by computers. If there is nothing much to go wrong, nothing much will go wrong. In extremes of temperature, the air-cooled 2CV survives where others do not; the push and pull gear rod may not be sophisticated, but is a useful place to rest your arm!

And, for the same price, what other car can you buy which offers 'convertible' driving with incredibly low fuel consumption, a car which can last virtually a life-time? The 2CV is undoubtably a legend. Its status of 'cult' vehicle cannot be denied, but it most certainly is a much loved and greatly enjoyed motoring experience. 'CITROEN 2CV' is designed to illustrate, with interesting pictures and surprising facts, that there is a lot more to this vehicle than an 'umbrella on four wheels!'

Thanks must go to many helpful and friendly Citroën lovers, too many to list here, but if your patience permits I give you just a few names:—
Barbara for her moral support and translation skills, Julian Leyton of Citroën UK Ltd, 2CVGB members including Simon Day, Jon Colley, Steve Hill, Peter Keeble, Jim Gibson, Roy Eastwood, Geoff Strutt; the BBC team of Howard Arnall, John King and David Lees; M. Roland Amadon and the Lempdes Comité des Fetes, officials and organisers at Berck-sur-Mer . . . my old friends Tim Parker and Tony Thacker; Geoffrey Clark for strengthening my back after my many long days of camera-carrying, Bernard Koppel for helping me to build a strong foundation . . . much praise to Arthur Williams, Citroën dealer of Crouch End, especially Sue and Mike; and to S. E. Thomas of Chiswick, the Kursaal Flyers and Will Mount.
And thanks to you for reading this book. I hope you enjoy it.

Atmosphere

France's scenery is vast and stunning . . . evocative light and colour blend with and enhance the rural landscapes.

To explore France—the 'hidden' France—there is no better way than to drive through its beautiful hill-top villages and wide-reaching panoramas in a leisurely and undemanding fashion. And there is no more satisfying way to discover the true flavour of the country than behind the wheel of a 2CV.

The once mastered quirky push/pull of the gear shift is as easy to operate as any other transmission. The willing engine breathes in the sweet smell of the vines and other, more familiar aromas of coffee and freshly-baked bread that are so typically French.

Undoubtedly the 2CV is a workhorse. Powering up long hard climbs or manoeuvring into tight corners creates an alarming roll, but roadholding is assured, with all four Michelin 'feet' firmly in contact with the ground. At the first sign of the summer sun, for that desirable bronzed look, just peel back the canvas roof and the whole car echoes the Mediterranean climate: luxury at an affordable price.

The 2CV, looking as plain or as pretty as its owner chooses, has never lacked the support of the French farmer for whom it was originally conceived. There is no doubt, therefore, that its use for hard labours, allied with its recreational capabilities, ensures its continuing great appeal.

In the city the driver would probably receive an unpleasant surprise in the form of a parking ticket or clamp, but in the hills of Provence at sunset, peace reigns.

Left

Aix-en-Provence is a provincial city with a traditional character. A cascading fountain greets visitors to the centre. A local 2CV owner hurries away from the dreaded yellow lines.

Right

A 2CV is easy to park once you gain confidence with the somewhat heavy steering. The wooden back-rest on the driver's seat must be welcome for those with back trouble, as the 2CV's seating can lead to a few aches and pains on long journeys.

Overleaf

A melon-seller, using the back of his Dyane as a pitch, is interrupted by the French equivalent of Morris dancers.

Left
2CV's can run on the highest octane rated fuel. One wonders if this distant 2CV is not powered by the miraculous Bandol grape.

Right
Aix-en-Provence and the Dirt Squad.

Overleaf main picture
Turn left at the sign of the cross. The French have faith in their cars.

Overleaf right
The number plate shows a lot of wear, but what about the van?

Toutes Directions

Centre Ville

POTERIE

Left
Mehari Azur at Bandol, southern France. A harbour location where luxury yachts adorn the sea-front. Air cooling is a big advantage in temperatures of over 35°C.

Right
A 2CV special negotiates the narrow back streets of Aix-en-Provence.

Overleaf left
The pretty driver and her Dyane are trend-setters! The car has always had an enthusiastic following, which is still maintained even after production stopped in 1982. Its extra comfort and refinements boosted Citroën's sales figures, but somehow the styling does not have that certain 'je ne sais quoi'.

Overleaf right
A Dyane corners with the inevitable Citroën roll but all is quite safe because of the unique suspension system.

Left
*An everyday scene in France.
Although the 2CV is a rarer sight in
cities its popularity is still enormous
with farmers and others living in
rural areas.*

F is for FRANCE.

Overleaf main picture
The busy autoroutes through France take their toll! Regular users of French motorways are familiar with the fees charged throughout their journey. However, most drivers balance these costs against first-class road surfaces and good maintenance. This Mehari appreciates the open road, but is happy to cruise at around 90 km/hour (56 mph) in the slow lane.

Overleaf insert
St Tropez has its share of crime and the heavy chain and padlock are a sensible precaution in open Meharis.

Left
Late evening in the French style.

Right
Silent Night.

Overleaf left
The French have acquired the knack of parking in secluded and cool places like this in Ramatuelle, a picturesque village in the hills a few kilometres behind St Tropez.

Overleaf right
A giant cockroach, or a slightly grotesque shadow of its former self? A 2CV sits alone in a French car park.

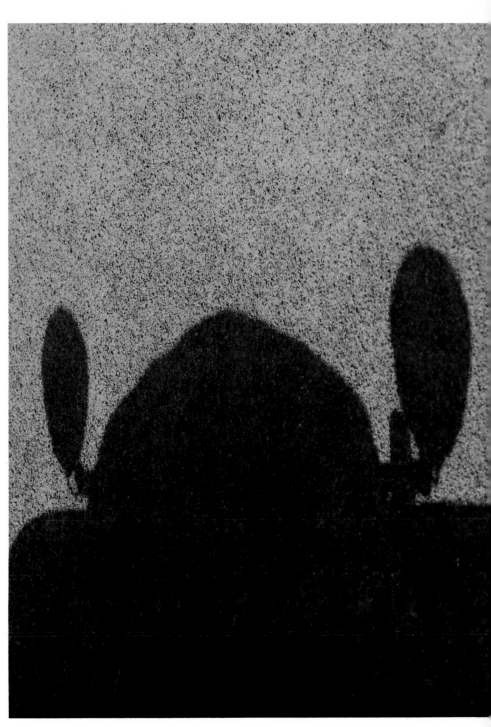

In the famous wine producing area of Bandol in Provence 2CV's are driven hard. It appears that this owner has a handy spares department in his own back garden.

Could this be the ultimate plumber's mate? Rusty and weatherbeaten vans or fourgonnettes like this 'classic' example prove that the type was bred for hard work.

On the eve of the 2CV's fortieth anniversary a plaque is fixed to the house where Pierre-Jules Boulanger, creator of the car, once lived in Lempdes.

French reflections

Above
What better way to idle away the tedium of a French traffic jam than through the roof of a patient Dyane. This one was spotted near Bandol in the South of France.

Right
Alexandra Palace now being re-built reminds us of not just BBC radio days but also boisterous and 'mind-blowing' rock concerts of the 1960's and '70's. This was the era when 2CV's and Harley-Davidsons shared grass (space) while their owners listened to the Rolling Stones or Pink Floyd.

Left
Late evening in an Essex pleasure dock. What better car for nipping down to the coast with family and friends?

Above
Working in the heat poses no problems for a Frenchman and his fourgonnette. Shorts for him and air-cooling for his van maintains the equilibrium.

Palm trees and telegraph poles form
a natural backdrop for an early 2CV,
a feature of which is the narrow
window space cut in the roof.

40 years on

In the small French village of Lempdes, a few kilometres east of Clermont-Ferrand, lived Pierre-Jules Boulanger, at the time Managing Director of the Citroën company which had been recently acquired by the huge Michelin group.

André Citroën, the pioneering car manufacturer, found economic pressure hard to bear. His insistence on building cars with style and panache did not fulfil the requirements of the rapidly changing conditions of the period. In 1935, having gone through a bankruptcy, Citroën's health failed and he died.

Boulanger was faced with the challenge of re-building the Citroën empire, on the basis of a product that even he could not have imagined would still be selling forty years and over 5 million (including variants) vehicles later—and, furthermore, from a design which has altered only slightly from its inception in 1948. The Michelin company could now field a clear rival to its famous German competitor, the VW 'Beetle'.

Under the guidance of Boulanger and his expert team, headed by Andre Lefebvre, work started on the TPV (*Toute Petite Voiture*) and the first working prototype appeared in 1937. The early models were very basic indeed, with the bodywork consisting of stretched linen!

The Second World War interrupted the development of the TPV, and it was decided to destroy all evidence of the project—except for one vehicle. German access to the TPV would have been a cruel blow, not only for Boulanger and

Spot the two horses.

his colleagues, but to national pride, for a car was being developed which promised—with more than a hint of eccentricity—to fulfil the working Frenchman's requirement for a functional, practical and economic method of transport. It was not until 1948, at the *Salon de l'Automobile*, that the 2CV re-surfaced as a 'real' motor car. However, the critical Press poured scorn on Citroën and their achievement, although the public benefited from good value motoring in the most basic of automobiles. In 1949 the 2CV became available to eager buyers, but economic restrictions by Government bodies controlled its sales, limiting them to priority users such as doctors and farmers.

However, as production increased at Levallois, Citroën could satisfy the needs each year of further thousands of buyers, culminating in 1966 in sales of over 160,000.

Since the launch of the 2CV, modern motoring has dictated different design concepts and driving requirements. Yet sales figures have remained buoyant, probably due in part to nostalgia for a bygone pioneering era. Although it is sad to reflect upon the closure of the Levallois factory and the transfer of production to more limited facilities in Mangualde, Portugal, there is no doubt that the few thousand 2CVs per year which are now sold, are going to good homes.

Lempdes, 'birthplace of the 2CV', was packed with visitors from as far afield as Japan, with dignitaries rubbing shoulders with enthusiasts and interested teenagers, in the celebrations to mark the 40th anniversary of the commercialisation of the 2CV.

Right
Citroën is always keen to introduce variations on a theme, and although the Bijou built at Slough attracted motorists on a budget they were not seen in great numbers. This French derived alternative speeds both its occupants along in prime comfort.

Right below
Through thick mist this beaming 2CV rapidly descends the hills of the Auvergne.

Below
Officials looking official and very French.

This 2CV is too good to eat! It is made from pastry and baked by a local master baker.

2CV prototype, 1936.

Right

In the village of Lempdes the static show for the anniversary celebrations included vehicles chosen for their dynamic characteristics. There is no doubting that this 'Safari' has seen the world many times over. The wire mesh covers and heavy duty 'nerf' bars keep unwanted obstacles at bay.

Overleaf

Camping at Lempdes, for some, is a pleasure. Extend the back of your 2CV to fit a bed or a kitchen—but watch out for the fuel tank when tossing crêpe flambé.

7th WORLD MEETING OF 2CV FRIENDS · JULY 25-28 1987 · ERICEIRA·P

507

I fly bleifrei

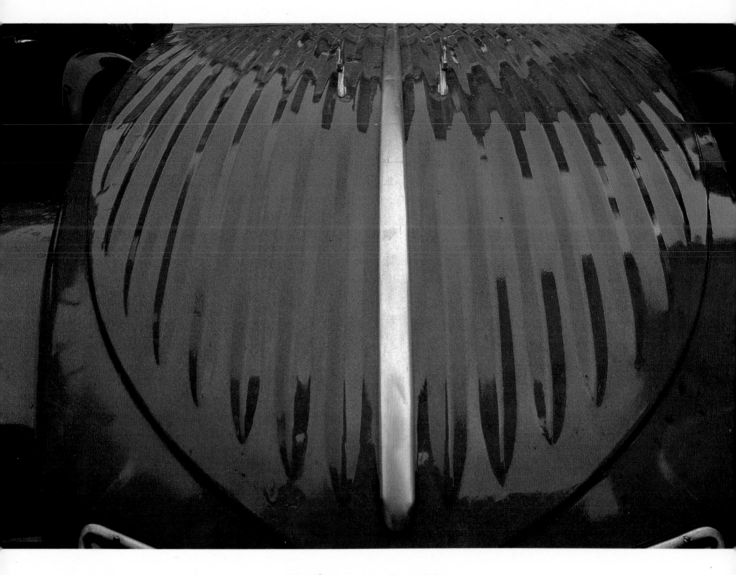

The ripple bonnet. Early 2CVs were
fitted with front-opening doors,
making dignified entry rather
difficult.

Above
Gitanes, Gaulois or Benson &
Hedges?

Overleaf left
*The famous 007 2CV driven by
'James Bond' was part of an
elaborate publicity programme by
Citroën. Note the bullet holes made
by plastic transfers. Every secret
agent should have one—after he
retires.*

Overleaf right
*A van from 'Psychedelia'. Obviously
well travelled owners who are used
to a home-away-from-home.*

The dealer, sales and service

Future sales of new 2CVs have been in question since the closure of the Levallois factory and transfer of production to Portugal: however, figures for some years to come appear to be healthy.

With most Citroën inspired advertising copy verging on the ridiculous, for example 'central locking' meaning that the driver can reach all handles from the inside without performing complex gymnastics: this car is not for the faint-hearted. The image of a car built for health fanatics and CND supporters has long out-grown the myth. The car is now more likely to be bought by young professionals as a back-up to the Porsche, as a second car by families who would rather have scratches on the 2CV than on the Jag, and by genuine Citroën enthusiasts who would drive nothing else.

For S. E. Thomas & Co., in Chiswick, West London, one of the capital's largest Citroën dealers, sales of 2CVs make an important contribution to turnover, and a visit to their showrooms is of great interest. Amongst sparkling turbos and diesels, 2CVs of every colour combination stand proudly, waiting to be driven away to their new homes.

Preparation and servicing are carried out by a large team of engineers and mechanics. After an initial service, however, the 2CV needs little maintenance. Service Manager Andy Craig suggests that its main appeal to both dealers and owners is its ease of maintenance, combined

Careful preparation removes all the unwanted grease and dirt from newly arrived cars into the workshop. Each vehicle is assured of personal attention by skilled mechanics in order to attract potential buyers. However, most 2CV's are sold prior to showroom display, such is the increasing demand.

with tried and tested service systems.

When the 2CV first embarked upon its illustrious career, it boasted only a 375 cc, flat twin air-cooled engine. It was not until 1970, when the 2CV6 was launched, that '602 cc' appeared on the bodywork, making it a real motor car!

Persuasive sales patter is extremely pertinent when describing the attractive features of a BX16-valve GTI, but only with straight talking can the successful sale of a 2CV be concluded. Current sales strategy regarding the '*deuche*' is tinged with some embarrassment, but with much humour. Sales brochures relating the adventures of Tin Tin, the famous cartoon character created by Hergé, conquering savage tribes in distant lands against unequal odds, and all because of the sheer grit and determination of the faithful Deux Chevaux is just one example of the self-mocking approach.

A beautiful 2CV6 Special or sophisticated Charleston can be in your proud ownership for a price between £4,000 and £4,500, complete with manufacturer's warranty and tax. A test drive is essential, as the first outing may be a mind-blowing experience, particularly with the top down! It is possible to hire one for a weekend. A dealer who entices new recruits into the Citroën family is Arthur Williams Ltd., in the North London borough of Hornsey, who offers either a green and white Dolly, or a single-tone blue. A weekend in the company of a 2CV may seriously improve your motoring enjoyment and whet your appetite for longer periods of fun.

Sales of 2CVs are not of course confined to Europe: the 2CV can be tracked down in the back streets of India or, even more surprisingly, on the great highways of the USA. Terry Keeton, based in Houston, Texas, manufactures 2CV replicas which meet all the latest safety and pollution requirements. Could this be the start of a whole new era for the deuche?

Looking down on these 2CV's one is reminded just how individual the Citroën is in today's style conscious marketplace.

Below
Up-to-date lighting on this modern Dolly.

Right
Suburban splendour.

Left
Curved and shaped glass makes a welcome change from modern streamlined designs.

Right
A large storage shelf runs across the front dashboard. Note the walking stick handbrake and the unusual push/pull gear rod.

Right below
Spaghetti junction. A few exposed wires here and there add to the car's charm?!

Left below
Window catches instead of handles: the bottom half of the glass flips and is caught—with practice!—in a nifty catch.

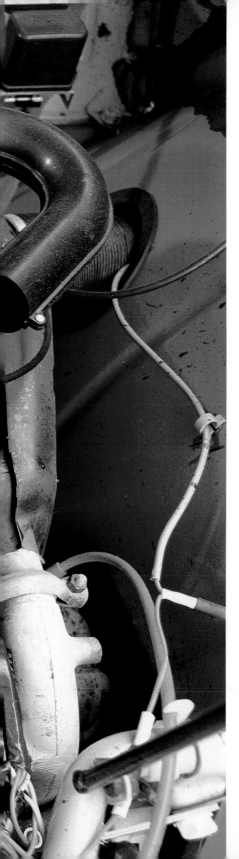

Overleaf left
The full 25-litres of fuel encased in these beautiful curves will take you many more miles than most cars twice the size.

Overleaf right
Everything for the Citroën! A strong corporate image is maintained even down to the green carpet tiles. An encouraging sign is the lack of oil trays underneath the cars

Left
Reliable and strong, the 602 cc air-cooled engine gives a maximum speed of 70 mph and fuel consumption of around 50 miles to the gallon at a constant 56 mph.

Below
Stripped to basics a body-less 2CV sits in Citroën's own training centre in Slough. It is ready for new engineering students to learn the fundamentals of 2CV motoring—keep it simple.

London to Brighton, the club scene

Early on Sunday morning in Battersea Park, London, the famous starting point for many car and commercial vehicle 'runs' to Brighton, Sussex, 2CVs of every colour, from all parts of Britain, arrive for a fun day of not too serious competition. The 'run' is always well attended, and between 300 and 600 cars usually participate. The atmosphere is always convivial, and it is a great opportunity to meet up with friends and fellow 2CVers.

The London to Brighton Run forms part of the club scene, which is very strong both in Britain and in Europe. Clubs have also been formed as far away as Japan and Australia, and world meetings are held on alternate years. The main function of these clubs is to promote friendship and understanding among enthusiasts of the unique 2CV character and life-style. Joining a club, whether it is the 2CVGB, the 2CV Club of Great Britain, or smaller local groups with interesting names, such as the Kursaal Flyers or the Thames Wheeldippers, is sure to bring a warm welcome from like-minded members.

The club calendar is full of enjoyable events such as 'raids' (a convoy of cars to picturesque destinations) or meetings at local pubs or social clubs. 2CV clubs also organise communal excursions to foreign meetings, taking advantage of reduced group rates for ferry or hovercraft crossings. The 2CVGB produces an informative and entertaining newsletter, and payment of the subscription launches a new

Lining up for the Brighton run. This car has to be noticed.

member into the world of ripple bonnets and crocodile hoods.

Meanwhile, back at Battersea Park, on a morning for which the weather forecast is 'cloudy, with chances or rain', 2CVs of every description wait patiently for the off. Cars line up in neat rows, with owners busy polishing and grooming their charges. The spirit of adventure—and 'belonging'—lives!

Small groups of cars head off through South London, passing waving groups of spectators through Brixton, then Croydon. Then—the rain. A far cry from the heat and dust of summer France. The only advantage was the longer than usual stop at the public house designated as the half-way point! But the trusty 2CV is more than able to cope with a downpour—as long as the de-mister (the passenger in the back with a strong arm and a cloth) is working.

Arrival at Preston Park in Brighton is, finally, in a blaze of sunshine. Parking is strictly for 2CVs, hundreds of them, arriving in long convoys, being herded into the car park, waiting on the damp grass for inspection by enthusiastic spectators . . .

Dozens of photographers with telephoto lenses, children with balloons, babies with frilly hats, bored dogs, all on a happy and sunny Sunday afternoon throng the park.

French cognac, I hope!

Left
How to be very British driving a very French car.

Left below
Mehari Plage at Brighton, East Sussex: owned by Geoff Strutt of the Thames Wheeldippers. Geoff and his wife are heavily involved in the club.

Right
A very neat 'Falcon' is in fact a well disguised 2CV. Coming in kit form, a transformation of this kind need not cost you a fortune, and you can be first off at the lights!

Right below
A 2CV prepared for rough roads, Brighton. This car has enough protection to allay the driver's fears of hitting unexpected obstacles.

Left
The 2CV's own fire brigade.

Above
An extreme case of colour coordination.

Overleaf left
Wet and horrible but roadholding is quite secure. Brighton is not too far, now.

Overleaf right above
Brighton or bust! This driver, complete with beret, scarf and beard has the right idea!

Overleaf right below
Come rain or shine this London to Brighton competitor noses his way out of a water-logged car park ready for the final section of the 'race'.

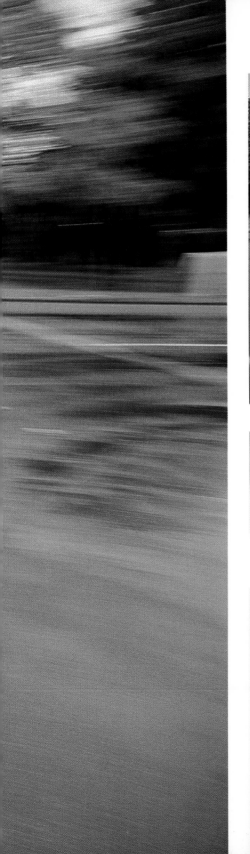

Previous pages right
This car runs on jungle juice.

Previous pages main picture
Remember the old Department of Transport safety slogan: Wear Something White At Night? Well, this is ridiculous, but in 2CV motoring 'anything goes' and red-chequered vans captures the imagination of fellow enthusiast.

Above
Another attractive Charleston.

Left
Let's do the Charleston! Available in two-tone grey or in black and red, the Charleston, launched in 1980, has proved very popular, and is now a trendy alternative to more up-to-date cars.

Above
Beautiful poppy-red Dyane at Brighton.

Overleaf left
At events and gatherings of enthusiasts artistic expertise abounds. A fourgonette receives the full treatment with a unique design engraved on the windows.

Overleaf right
Steve Hill builds high-performance racing cars, not for cross country but for Europe's flat racing circuits. Le Mans-style 24-hour endurance events for 2CV's may well be on their way to Britain and judging by the looks of this lovely car they should prove a crowd-puller.

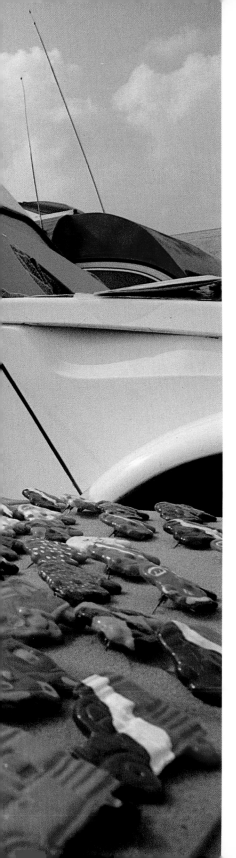

This neat umbrella matches the colour of the Dolly's seat covers. An immaculate car owned by the Broadribbs of South Wales.

Above
A Grand Prix style line-up at Battersea Park. The goal is not so much to reach Brighton in the shortest time, but to reach Brighton!

This car has plenty of fans at Brighton's Preston Park. Note the ingenious use of metal tubing neatly supporting the headlights and strengthening the engine compartment.

Above
Ian McCleave, David Gale, David
Chapman and Kevin Biffin embellish
a rare Beachcomber, a limited
edition vehicle introduced in Great
Britain in 1984. Driver and
passengers are founder members of
the 'Kursaal Flyers', an Essex club
which was formed after the 1987
London to Brighton run. Pictured in
France, their superb car is well
prepared.

Right
At least somebody is laughing at the
dire conditions. Maybe that drink
was the key? (Strictly Coca-Cola).

Racing and climbing (2CV Cross)

The lure of speed and competition has led to the marvellous specatacle of 2CV-cross racing. A sport for only the most iron-stomached individual, where tearing around dirt and dust tracks at top speeds is the norm. The incredible sight of twenty or more Citroëns racing double chevron to double chevron, bumping and edging their way through the 'traffic' is an exciting event for driver and spectator alike.

2CV-cross racing is now, however, confined mainly to Europe, with meetings in France throughout the summer months.

It is a family event, with dad or mum entering specially-prepared race cars in heats, semi-finals and finals. Having in many cases driven long distances to participate, on arrival tents are pitched, tools, parts and spares are gathered, and last-minute mechanical adjustments are made for the coming races. The competition is fierce, but so is the camaraderie, as this is still very much a fun sport. However, motor racing of any sort is dangerous, and there are strict safety regulations and provisions for both drivers and spectators. Marshals are posted at each bend, equipped and ready with appropriate signal flags, extinguishers and cutting gear.

The shock of seeing a 2CV hurtling through the air, somersaulting and coming to rest on its 'head', is even more surprising when the driver coolly regains gravity and

Under normal conditions the 2CV is surprisingly stable (although it often does not appear to be). The key to the ride is its unusual suspension system: four main springs mounted front and back operate in a concertina manner, softening harsh braking, bumps and tight corners. Today's driving conditions are just a little too tricky for this to be effective!

fires his motor to try to win back his or her race position.

One such race meeting is held annually at Berck-sur-Mer, 20 kms from Boulogne. As easy crossing via Dover attracts British interest, although the entrants are predominantly French. It is definitely worth the journey. The racing has to be the closest in motor sport, with the excitement continuing throughout each race. Cars accelerate down the straight, battling for pole position at the first corner. Tearing through the gears, each driver fights to control the car over treacherous surfaces. What might be a smooth track on lap one soon deteriorates into a bumpy minefield of ditches and holes waiting to capture the wheels of an unlucky participant. A wheel catches in a deep rut—and instantly the vehicle leaves the ground, hurtling through the air and bouncing into the oncoming cars. Somehow the rest of the pack motors through obstacles like this as though on a leisurely Sunday drive . . . but suddenly sounds of metal against metal fill the air, and car after car pile into the one in front, creating a concertina of *deuches*, until the marshals run to free cars and drivers from the melee. Nobody is hurt—in fact, the only injury is to the driver's fierce pride!

At a slightly slower pace, but with even greater bravado, drivers practise the art of hill-climbing in purpose-built four-wheel drive 2CVs. The vehicles, which are especially prepared for such daredevil feats, charge up and down incredibly steep gradients, to the delight of excited onlookers.

The 4 × 4 vehicle varies in its specification, from twin-engined dirt buggy to the most beautifully-prepared powerhouse. One has to marvel at the heroic attempts of car and driver to conquer a hill of slippery grass and rocks. The basic idea at such impromptu 4 × 4 demonstrations is to reach the summit of any chosen 'mountain' in a style reminiscent of kamikaze pilots during the war. Almost all make it to the top, often through sheer determination.

Two racing Frenchmen, holding up the lightweight bonnet, who are about to do battle in a fire red racer. The 'belly' pan of the car at the front prevents flying debris from penetrating the engine.

Overleaf main picture
Incidents of this kind show the inherent strength of a 2CV body. Driver and car re-started the race within moments of the unrehearsed pause.

Overleaf above
Specially modified vehicles have their own race. Unfortunately, even this 'mini' has problems escaping the depths of soft sand. The twin-engined vehicle behind is well and truly banjaxed.

Overleaf below
Mud in your eye.

More amiable 2CV competitors.

Cut-down 2CV handles 1-in-6 slope with ease. The roll-over bar looks solid but there is some doubt about the washing lines.

Left
Didier has a healthy spread of sponsors.

Right
The chassis of the racing 2CV can be considerably modified for competition. All the glass is taken out and a fine wire mesh protects the driver from flying debris. Rear doors are removed, lights and electrics are kept to a bare minimum. Essential engine straps hold the bonnet firmly closed. The roof normally consists of a small piece of metal welded above the driving position, and a strong roll-over bar protects amazingly well.

Overleaf right above
Beach buggy racer. Metal tube frame is a welcome necessity.

Overleaf right below
Four-wheel drive Citroëns can negotiate all terrains, but a willing passenger is often of great assistance.

Overleaf main picture
The metal 'belly', as in rally prepared cars, takes constant punishment, but keeps the chassis in one piece and protects the 25-litre fuel tank.

Under normal driving conditions the Michelin 125–15X tyres are inflated to around 28 lb per square inch. For exceptional terrain 135 Michelins are normally fitted and may be inflated to 32 psi or deflated to 9 psi for very soft sand or earth.

The 2CV's flexibility of body/chassis and mechanics is certainly an important reason for its justified popularity and transformations into so many different versions.

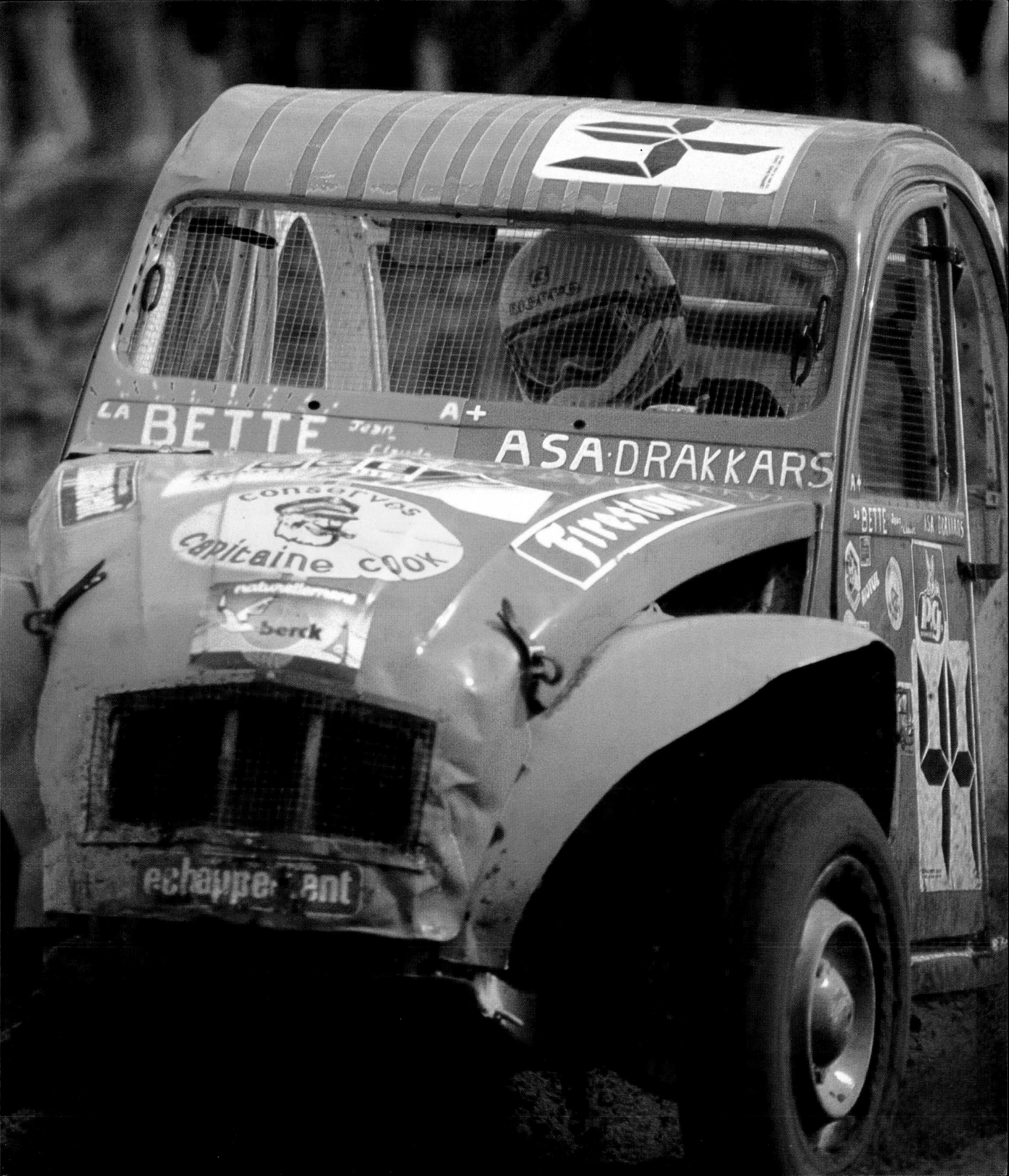
LA BETTE
A+
ASA·DRAKKARS
conserves
Capitaine COOK
berck

A little rusty around the edges but a good advertisement for the race.

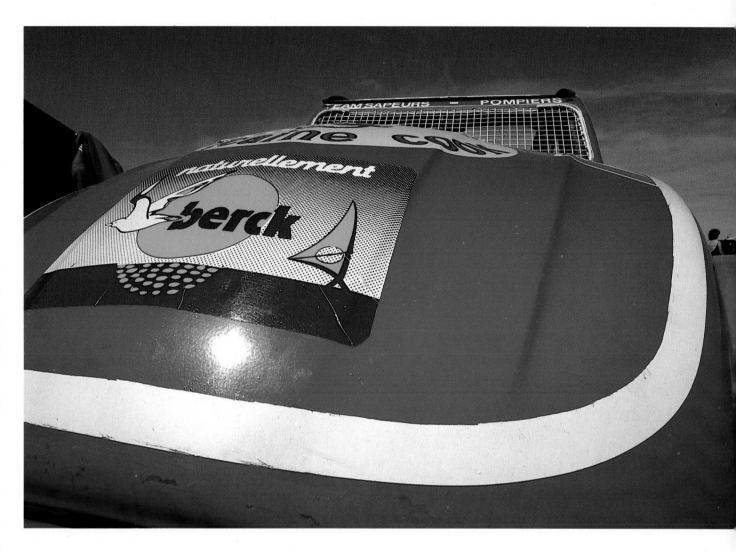

The municipality of Berck pointing
out emphatically the other
attractions of the town apart from
crazy motor sports.

Overleaf
*Close contact racing at speed seen
on 'German autobahns' creates a
spectacle equal to the most closely
fought Formula I Grand Prix, and is
probably just as draughty!*

'This is the BBC'

In a remote corner of Derbyshire, on a dull, drizzly and windy August day, a British Broadcasting Corporation recording unit assembles for a day of intense work.

Their task is to capture on video tape a scene from the series, 'Shadow of the King', directed by Matthew Robinson and featuring David Schofield and Georgina Coombes.

Led by John King, the Outside Broadcast team is a professional, no-nonsense crew and makes recording difficult scenes seem easy, due to the good organisation of each member of the production unit, the actors and the director.

With rough terrain and steep gradients to contend with, the production called for smooth camera-work, combined with mobility. We all know the answer! A new (Portugal-made) 2CV was chosen by the transport division for its silken ride and flexibility, and with the aid of rigger/driver Clive Treacher and cameraman Trevor Wimlett, the car succeeded in a steady work-flow throughout the day.

Once the back of the car is off, there are not too many places to hold on to, although everybody arrived in one piece.

Howling winds make life hazardous for crew and car.

After a 'dummy' run-through of the
scene, car and actors return to the
start position, ready for the take.
The heavy red cable from the video
camera leads straight into the
recording equipment, all mounted on
board the 2CV.

Beauty and the Beast (and the best of the rest)

If André Citroën was alive today, one wonders if he might scream in horror or smile with praise at some of the wild but wonderful customised 2CVs that bear his name.

Multi-coloured designs adorn metallic paintwork; lowered suspension, chromed engines and chopped bodies all sound a bit radical, but this is where individual style wins the day.

Yet even a two-tone factory paint finish creates a car which stands out in a crowd: even in its 'stock' state it attracts the attention—and envy?—of many.

Although the 2CV is nicknamed, amongst numerous other titles, 'The Ugly Duckling', some owners prefer to show the car in a different light. Engines are exchanged or 'beefed up', perhaps even a powerful turbo dropped into position. This time it is the '*deuche*' which leaves the others standing.

Extreme care must be taken when manoeuvring a standard or custom 2CV, as the bodywork is paper-thin, but re-modelling tends to consist of bolt-on bodywork or beautiful—and original—artwork. Regular visitors to campsites often convert the rear of the car into a mini-kitchen or sleeping area by removing the rear seats—or some prefer a buggy-type convertible.

Chop the top off, neaten the edges and wait for the sun to shine! Nor are large sums of money necessary. New slip-on seat covers, thick pile carpet and snazzy steering-wheels can transform your 2CV and upgrade it to luxury status!

Zebra with lights.

To be original in the world of the 2CV is always a challenge, but the choice and possibilities are endless. Citroën have manufactured many variants on the two horse-power theme, and these have included twin-engined four-wheel drives, open-top fun vehicles and a few real ugly ducklings and other oddities. You may choose a plastic-bodied Mehari for the beach, or an Acadiane van for transporting spoils gathered on a Continental driving trip.

The 'Lomax' and 'Falcon' are names of kit cars which are easy to build. Both are fashioned around the same 2CV frame and running gear, with the ever-popular 602 cc air-cooled engine.

The Dyane, launched in 1968 as an up-market car, has different styling, a flatter nose and less radical curves. The policy of using existing mainframe and engine parts paid off for Citroën, as by 1983, when production ceased, 1,400,000 Dyanes had been sold. A Dyane is as welcome as any to the 2CV fraternity, but the strange sight of a rare Ami or Bijou surprises all but the most hardened enthusiasts. The Ami could not be more ugly or the Bijou more odd.

Beauty contestants and show cars are among this next section of pictures collected at events in France and Great Britain.

Vivid red car with twin headlights speeds along the autoroute near Lempdes.

Futuristic paint-work at Paddock Wood, Kent.

Smoked glass hides a roll-over bar,
complete with extinguisher. The
large exhaust reveals that this car is
not 'stock'.

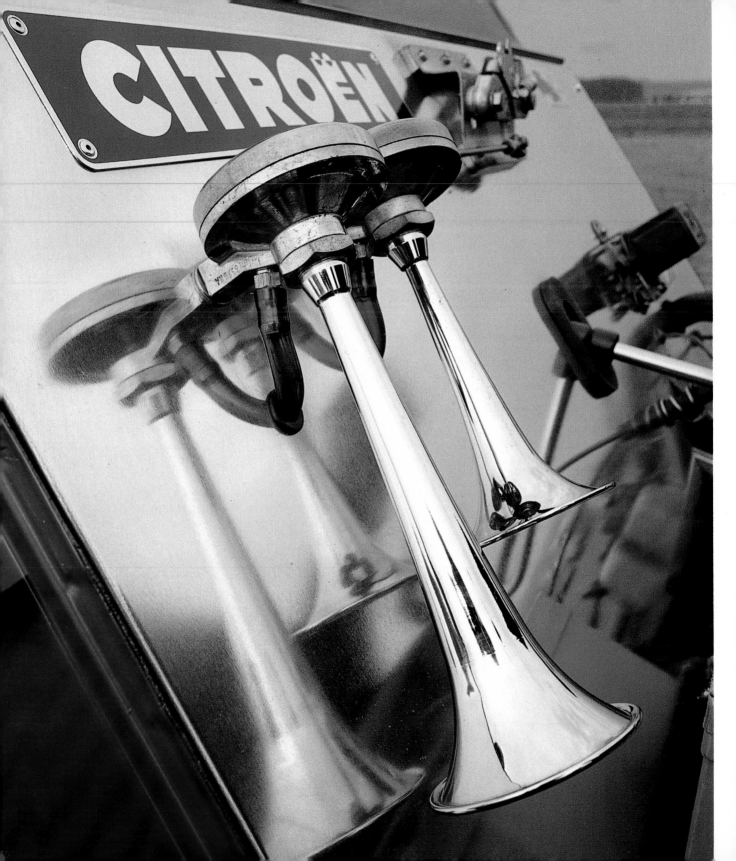

The bonnet of the Ducruet s brothers custom beauty lifts off to reveal skillful detailing.

Below
The owner has made good use of 'classic' brass pipework. Commendation is due for the time and effort needed to achieve these outstanding results.

Left
Two-tone Klaxon.

THE 2 CV CENTRE
Chadwick End
☎ LAPWORTH 3404

2CV owners are renowned for their ingenuity and humour. A back-to-front deuche must win the prize for originality. Daryl Stokes runs a 2CV centre in Lapworth, and decided to dream up a bizarre car that looks crazy but it totally functional. Due to his imagination, the Press was able to fill valuable copy space: a publicity campaign which brought results.

The Bijou is a rare car. A town
vehicle which did not prove popular.

Left
A mobile kitchen gives independence: neat, functional and out of the way, complete with fluorescent lighting. The Americans have huge 40-foot mobile homes. European counterparts make do with 3830 (millimetres) of moving convenience.

Above
Remove the window frames, paint the car and add a few multi-coloured spots for an almost legally drivable 2CV. Ideal for coastal driving, but not at night as there appear to be some lighting problems.

Above
'Jaune mimosa' is one of those car
colours which linger in the memory,
set off by friendly owners Julia and
Martyn Yates. A classic example of
absolute enthusiasm, down to the
miniature Michelin man. Members
too of the 'Lancashire Hot-Pots' club,
the Yates are regular European
travellers, accompanied often by
their children, dogs and guitars.

Right
Just to show what can be added to
your favourite Mehari. This looks
like complete self-sufficiency for the
'around the world' enthusiast.

Above
Is it a VW?

Right
*Boot extensions are street-legal
accessories which can hold the
essential of life.*

Jean-Luc and Alain Ducruet own a
customising and renovating business
in Cruseilles, and this chef d'oeuvre,
originally a fourgonnette which had
been chopped, cut, lowered, flamed,
and chromed, attracted a great deal
of attention at the celebrations in
Lempdes.

*Side view, showing metallic flames
and black covers for lights.*

Above
No marks for perfection but the 'foot' rest is neat.

Left
Cloth seats soften the ride and the diamond pattern improves the aesthetics.

Right above
An example of what can be done with imagination. The wings are bolted on, and the lowered chassis signifies radical changes. This white beauty was seen in France.

Right
Chromed excellence.

Overleaf left
When well engineered and expertly fitted, as in this splendid 2CV, bolt-on fibreglass body parts can look alluring and invite much admiring commentary from passersby.

Overleaf right
Art for art's sake.

Above
Traction avant?, or has the 2CV 'thoughts above its stations'?

Left
British and French collaboration, or wishful thinking? A Jaguar/Citroën is an interesting concept but highly unlikely. A pet Jaguar from a local tourist zoo gamely poses on a soft top.

Right
Belle Epoque, winner of the Lempdes beauty contest. Denis and Marielle Jean of Bizanos, south-west France, have owned this 2CV since 1983. Originally green, it is now an immaculate pearl grey. The bonnet is cribbed from a 1957 model, and other additions date from 1958. The windscreen is fashioned in two pieces, an unusual departure from tradition. Wire wheels (usually inserts) and beautifully maintained bodywork made sure that this car was the first choice of the judges (the mayor of Lempdes and his entourage).

Overleaf
Checking wind resistance in a swish Cabriolet.